T0145048

"Keep trying. Keep believing in yourself. Hopefully,
you will have somebody believe in you."
John H. Johnson

For the believers, future entrepreneurs, innovators,
creatives, and dream achievers -
Angela F. Courtney

He was born Johnny Johnson in the rural segregated southeast Arkansas Delta. Johnny grew up to become John H. Johnson and the first Black person named to Forbes 400 list of richest Americans.

He was the founder, chairman and publisher of Johnson Publishing Company.

Angela F. Courtney captures Johnson's story in a unique way focusing on his childhood on the banks of the Mississippi River, when he was nine years old.

Vivid illustrations portray Johnson's boyhood life when Johnson and his mother lived on the Arkansas Levee for six weeks during the 1927 flood.

Mississippi River

Arkansas Levee

4

John H. Johnson was a pioneering visionary and trailblazing businessman. But before he became John H. Johnson, he was just Johnny.

The great grandson of slaves, Johnny was born in a shotgun tin roofed house in Arkansas City, Arkansas, three blocks from the Mississippi River. He was born into great adversity and extreme poverty; but he was richly loved and encouraged by both his parents. His mother, Mrs. Gertrude "Gert" Johnson Williams was born August 4, 1891, in Arkansas City's neighboring Lake Village. She married Richard Lewis and gave birth to her first child, Beulah. The marriage ended, and she later married Leroy Johnson, Johnny's father. She was God-fearing and revered the Lord. She had a third-grade education, but valued education and taught Johnny the importance of self-sufficiency, perseverance, hard work, and integrity. Johnny's mother had several miscarriages before Johnny was born. She prayed to God that if He would give her another child, she would devote her life to giving that child a better life. Johnny was born shortly after midnight, January 19, 1918.

"Her body was in the fields and kitchen, but her mind was in another places, in the first-class section."

Johnny's mother worked as a housekeeper. "She was active in the church and in service organizations."

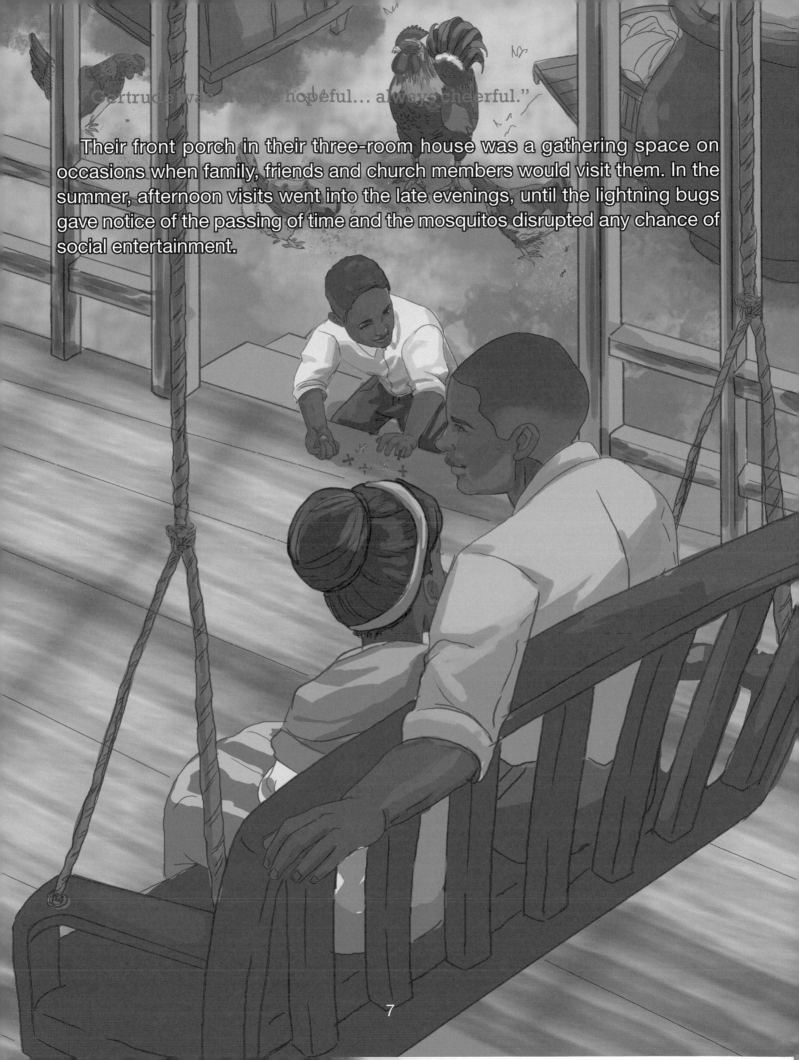

"Gertrude was always hopeful... always cheerful."

Their front porch in their three-room house was a gathering space on occasions when family, friends and church members would visit them. In the summer, afternoon visits went into the late evenings, until the lightning bugs gave notice of the passing of time and the mosquitos disrupted any chance of social entertainment.

"I didn't have a lot of toys. I didn't have a lot of clothes. But I had a lot of love."

To break up the constant boredom of the usual games - tag, hide and seek, marbles, pick-up sticks, jump rope, horseshoes, hopscotch, and catch ball, Johnny and his friends used their imagination to create games.

The Delta's moist heat drenching Johnny's clothes could not discourage him and his neighborhood friends from playing. The boys rolled in the grass, catching an itch to their already dry skin. Not even the crawdads, wild rabbits, or the Mississippi River rodents that found their way onto the neighbors' yards could distract Johnny and his friends from enjoying the outdoors.

The boys laughed with innocence, while discovering pure joy sharing their gently-used games and homemade toys.

The sprinkles of water gushing from the water pump were welcoming as Johnny and his friend refreshed a bucket of water to ease the thirst of the sun on their burning skin.

"I have a great respect for mothers."

"J-o-h-n-n-y!" his mom, pronouncing each vowel and consonant in his name, yelled. Johnny's back was against the sound of her voice. It was almost time for dinner.

"Come inside", his mom exclaimed.

"Yes, ma'am," Johnny replied, stopping for a moment to let his mother know his plans. Then he took off hurriedly to be with his friends for one last chance to be outside before their day of activities came to an end.

"It's important to have someone in life who believes in you."

Johnny's dad traveled a lot. Johnny didn't see him often. His dad followed the levee camps up and down the Mississippi River.

"My mother was a God-fearing woman who believed we ought to treat people the way we wanted to be treated."

♪ ♪ ♪ ♪ ♪ ♪

Swing low, sweet chariot coming for to carry me home
Swing low, sweet chariot coming for to carry me home
I looked over Jordan and what do I see, coming for carry me home
A band of angels coming after me
Coming for to carry me home ♪ ♪ ♪ ♪ ♪ ♪

When Johnny was eight years young, his dad was killed in a sawmill accident.

The next year, following the sawmill accident with Johnny's father, Johnny's mother married James Williams. Mr. Williams worked for a bakery shop delivering groceries.

There is a wisdom in the body that is older and more reliable than clocks and calendars."

Johnny's stepfather was a good dad to him. They never had a "cross" word.

Of the few times when there was a disagreement between the two, they spoke with Johnny's mother to let her know of their opposite viewpoints.

They took turns sharing their thoughts on a subject they had strong opinions about.

Johnny's mom was the authority in the family, and the one who disciplined. She used a switch to emphasize her teaching.

At times, she would make Johnny go into the backyard and cut a switch or branch from a tree.

Johnny would always get a small one and his mother would send him back to get a bigger and stronger branch.

"My mother was the influence in my life. She was strong and had great faith in the ultimate triumph of justice and hard work. She believed passionately in education."

One day, Johnny wanted his mother's attention to solve a dispute with his stepfather. The family sat at the dinner table together, when Johnny began to speak to his mother about his stepfather. With a timid but clear tone to emphasize his point, Johnny said, "Mother, tell Mr. Williams to stop doing that."

With a brief glance at Johnny, then in the direction of his wife, in a matter-of-fact southern gentleman's voice, Johnny's stepfather said calmly, "Gertrude, tell Johnny, I don't like that."

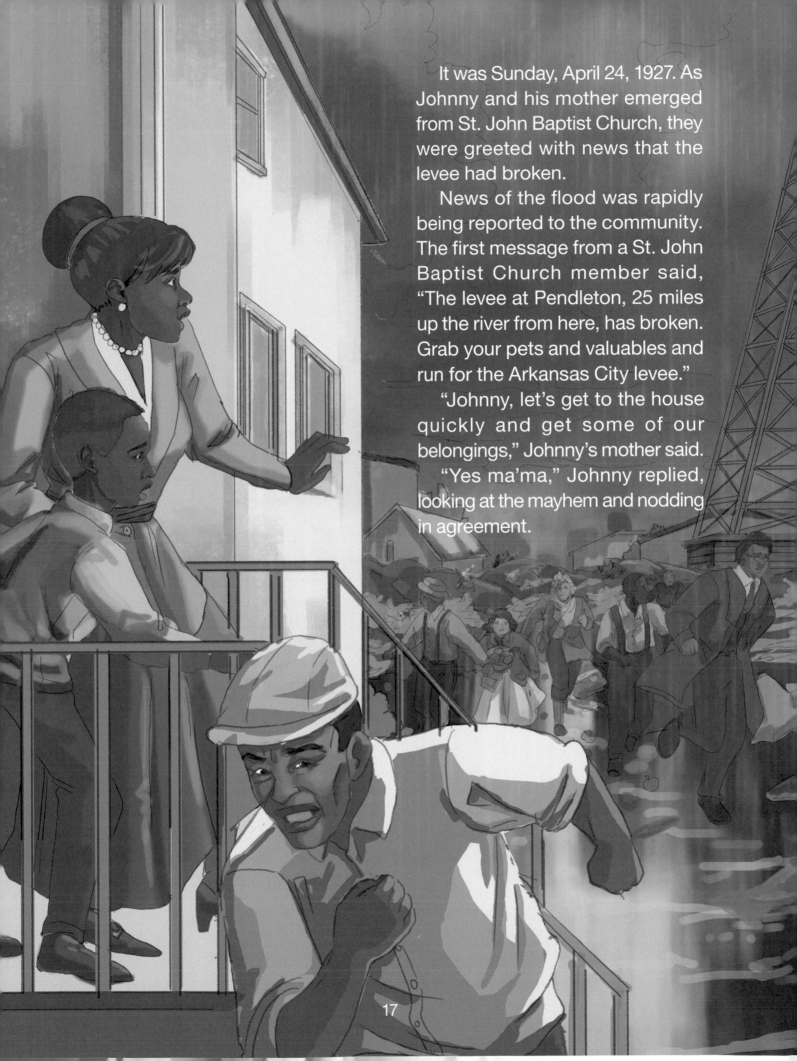

It was Sunday, April 24, 1927. As Johnny and his mother emerged from St. John Baptist Church, they were greeted with news that the levee had broken.

News of the flood was rapidly being reported to the community. The first message from a St. John Baptist Church member said, "The levee at Pendleton, 25 miles up the river from here, has broken. Grab your pets and valuables and run for the Arkansas City levee."

"Johnny, let's get to the house quickly and get some of our belongings," Johnny's mother said.

"Yes ma'ma," Johnny replied, looking at the mayhem and nodding in agreement.

17

St. John Baptist Church was relocated to
Morning Star Street after the flood of 1927.

The second message, minutes later came from an Arkansas City neighbor saying, "Forget the valuables and pets. Run for your lives!"

"We have to get to safety on top of the levee," Johnny's mom exclaimed firmly.

Johnny's mom was trying not to show her disbelief of the raging water.

"Keep up with me, Johnny, keep up with me!" Johnny's mother called out.

"We need to get to the levee, we need to get to the levee fast!" Johnny's mother repeated with urgency in her voice.

The water was coming behind them. Dogs were barking. People were screaming.

Johnny running, struggling to catch his breath, asked his mother, "Are we going to make it, mom?" She gripped his hands tighter.

"Mom, will the water swallow us?" Johnny asked anxiously.

Johnny was terrified and doubtful that they would not make it to safety.

Johnny's mom then shifted into a higher gear to get to the top of the levee.

"We are going to make it mom!" Johnny exclaiming with his eyes looking away from the rising water.

"And I remember, as if it was yesterday, the shock as I opened my eyes on a scene of interracial bedlam."

"Hands, I remember the hands – black, white, brown, yellow hands- reaching out to us, pulling us to safety."

"Take my hand," one person said reaching toward someone.

"Grab my arm!" Another person pulled at several other people.

"You are almost there," another encouraging voice said, tugging to get as many bodies as possible to on top of the levee.

"From time-to-time, rabbits, quails, deer and even foxes emerged from the water and scrambled over the manmade hills of furniture and clothes."

"Mom, I'm cold." "I'm scared, mom," Johnny said.
Johnny's mom comforted him, amid her own fears.
"Help is on the way, Johnny. Don't worry about a thing," she said, reassuring him and believing that God would send the government to help everyone."

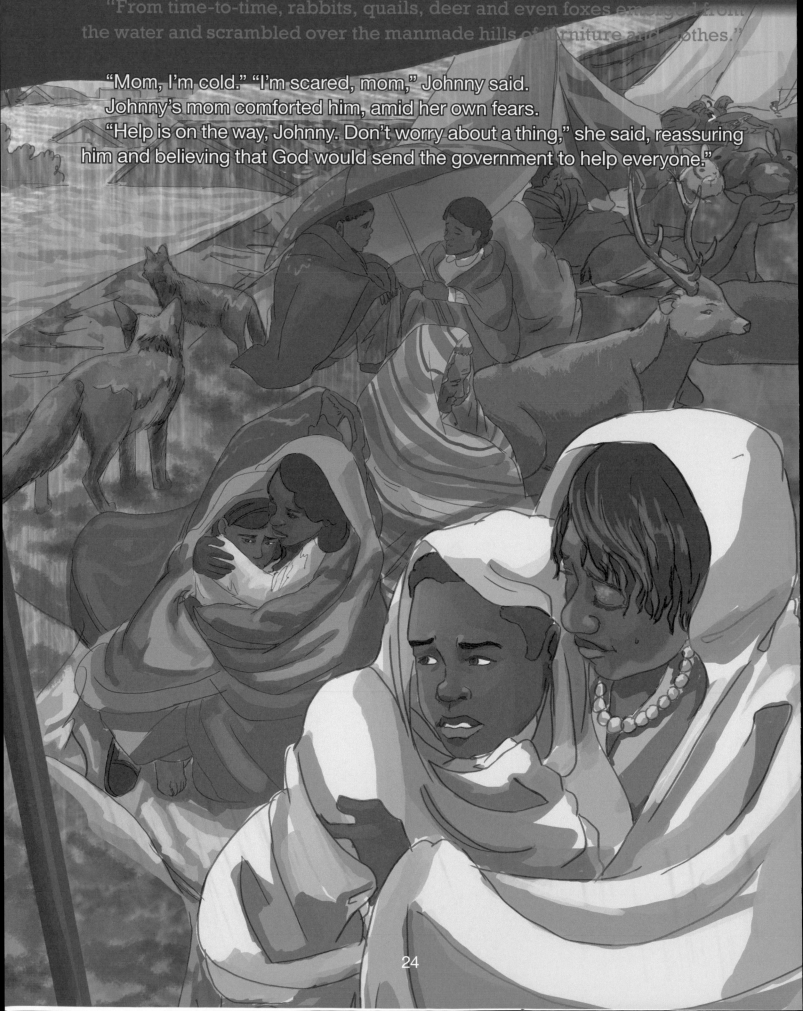

"And I soon perceived that there were things to be seen on this levee that a nine-year old boy had never seen."

Johnny watchfully observing everyone and everything, looks down from the levee to try and get a glimpse of their home.

"Do you think our house is gone forever?" Johnny asked with uncertainty hoping for his toys to withstand the flood as much as their house.

His mother weary, but ever so faithful, responded. "Our house will surface. We will find our house," she said though uncertainty lingered in her thoughts.

"... Everything we owned – our clothes, our furniture and the few dollars we'd saved – was gone."

"The authorities had promised to build new homes for families who couldn't find their old houses. But we were unlucky. We found our house, battered and full of dirt and nameless things that crawled, and slithered, three blocks away."

Johnny saw the adults working and wanted to help in any way he could. "Mom, may I help the grownups?" Johnny asked with excitement. "Yes, Johnny. Just be careful and don't go too far away where I can't see you," Mrs. Gertrude said.

"… The Mississippi River, more powerful than the 14th Amendment, more powerful even than the churches of Jesus Christ, had washed away the sin of division and that Blacks and Whites were working together and fighting the Mississippi River together, shoulder to shoulder."

"They gave me a chance to shovel and hand them sandbags, and the work wasn't that bad," Johnny said.

Johnny's mom praised him for being a big help on the levee. "Johnny, we are all in this situation together and everyone helping is making a difference. I'm very proud of you Johnny."

As the water receded and the cleaning up was completing, Johnny, his mother and all the residents were relieved as they began rebuilding a life after the flood down the levee in Arkansas City.

"Mom, we can walk in the mud to get home, can't we? We are going home now, mom, aren't we?" Johnny asked.

"Yes, we are going home now," his mother promised him.

"The boy on the levee was the father of the man and the publisher."

30

Johnny's mother taught him about God's love and treating everyone the way he wanted to be treated.

The six weeks on the Mississippi River Levee taught Johnny about people. It gave him a sense of working together to achieve a common goal. It taught him that when people treat everyone equally and the same – as his mother taught him – everyone succeeds.

Life on the Mississippi River Levee also taught Johnny to believe. Believe you will see better and brighter days. Believe you will be able to get to the next level in life. Believe that the future has great possibilities. Believe. Just believe. And with optimism, faith, hard work and integrity, "someone will hopefully believe in you."

TIMELINE OF EVENTS

The original boyhood home of Johnny Johnson was transitioned from Weatherwood Street, the street Johnny and his family lived on, next to the Desha County Courthouse in Arkansas City, Arkansas. During the move of Johnny's boyhood home, the house collapsed due to complications caused by the 1927 flood.

The establishment of John H. Johnson Cultural and Educational Museum (John H. Johnson Museum) was initiated by the University of Arkansas Pine Bluff (UAPB). UAPB is a Historically Black College and University (HBCU) within the University of Arkansas System. John H. Johnson Museum is a partnership with Arkansas City, Desha County, and UAPB. John H. Johnson Museum, a replica museum of Johnny's boyhood home is located in the historic district of Arkansas City.

In 2004, John H. Johnson returned to his boyhood home for the dedication of the John H. Johnson Museum.

In 2019, Friends of John H. Johnson Museum became curators of John H. Johnson Museum and John H. Johnson Day.

On April 19, 2019, the 92nd Arkansas General Assembly, at the request of Friends of John H. Johnson Museum, enacted legislation for John H. Johnson Day, to become a November 1st statewide memorial holiday, honoring John H. Johnson.

On November 2, 2021, U.S. Congressman Danny Davis, at the request of Friends of John H. Johnson Museum, recognized John H. Johnson with a resolution in the United States House of Congress.

On November 1, 2023, Arkansas Department of Parks, Heritage and Tourism, division of Arkansas State Parks dedicated a commemorative plaza and the first statue in the world in John H. Johnson's honor in his hometown of Arkansas City, Arkansas.

CREDITS

Succeeding Against The Odds
The Autobiography of a Great Businessman
John H. Johnson with Lerone Bennett, Jr.
©1989 by John H. Johnson and
Lerone Bennet, Jr., 1989, 1992

EBONY® The John H. Johnson Interview
The Inspiring Last Interview Of
Ebony and Jet Founder, Publisher and Chairman
John H. Johnson
His compelling Life, Ideas and Achievement
In His Own Words
©2007, Johnson Publishing Company

ABOUT THE AUTHOR

Angela F. Courtney is the volunteer curator for the John H. Johnson Museum (www.johnhjohnsonmuseum.org), and John H. Johnson Day. John H. Johnson Day was established during the 92nd Arkansas General Assembly and is observed annually November 1st. Angela established Friends of John H. Johnson Museum to curate the life and legacy of John H. Johnson. She is a former University of Arkansas Pine Bluff adjunct professor. She received her BA degree from the University of Arkansas Little Rock and her MA degree from Webster University. She has worked and volunteered abroad, including serving in mission-based work in South Africa. She is the executive director and founder of Alex Foundation (www.alex-foundaton.org), a nonprofit organization that introduces students to architecture and design, including through place-based education by exploring historic and heritage-based buildings and structures of cultural relevance and significance.

Printed in the United States
by Baker & Taylor Publisher Services